Pendle

witch country

Vertebrate Publishing, Sheffield
www.v-publishing.co.uk

'She liued in the Forrest of Pendle, amongst this wicked company of dangerous Witches.'

– *The Wonderfull Discoverie of Witches in the Countie of Lancaster*, Thomas Potts, 1613

For Carol Carysforth

who believed in the magic within us all.

First published in 2019 by Vertebrate Publishing.
VERTEBRATE PUBLISHING
Crescent House, 228 Psalter Lane, Sheffield S11 8UT, United Kingdom.
www.v-publishing.co.uk

This book is a work of non-fiction. The author has stated to the publishers that, except in such minor
respects not affecting the substantial accuracy of the work, the contents of the book are true.

A CIP catalogue record for this book is available from the British Library.

ISBN: 978-1-911342-95-3 (Hardback)

10 9 8 7 6 5 4 3 2 1

Written, photographed and designed by Alastair Lee – www.alastairleephotography.co.uk
Production by Vertebrate Publishing – www.v-publishing.co.uk

Vertebrate Publishing is committed to printing on paper from sustainable sources.

Printed and bound in China by Latitude Press Ltd.

HALF-TITLE PAGE – An avenue of trees and hedge-rows creates an evocative image in the autumn light; a horseback rider wouldn't be out of place on this path found near Roughlee. PREVIOUS PAGES – An iridescent Pendle Hill at first light. Shafts of light in the Ribble Valley. Clearing mists from Pendle Hill. Mist lingers in the Salter-foth valley. Pendle Hill from Weets. Pendle's big end. Mist burns over a Pendle farmhouse. THIS PAGE – The fringe of a westerly weather front moves over East Lancashire at sunrise on a late November morning. Captured from the summit of Weets Hill.

A Dark Corner

Pendle is an area best known for its association with the controversial witch trials of 1612; a damp, dark corner of East Lancashire. It is a modest location overshadowed by the grandeur of the tourist-laden Lake District to the north, while to the north-east the famous peaks and caves of the Yorkshire Dales draw the crowds. To the south it is simply ignored in favour of its close relations in the Peak District. However, this isolated outlier of an uprising in the landscape has seen it all. It has weathered battles, withstood invasions, survived witchcraft, witnessed religious visions and scientific experiments. It's even overseen a revolution of the industrial kind. These once-wild hills on the road to nowhere remain resolute for those that hold the landscape close to their hearts. The area now known as the Forest of Pendle, with its centrepiece being the outstanding Pendle Hill, is not a location that springs to mind when we think of classic English natural wonders. What we shall see in the pages that follow are lands not only worthy of their title of Area of Outstanding Natural Beauty, but a place of great variety, a microcosm of everything that is quintessentially English about a landscape: subtle, impassive, atmospheric, beautiful, at times spectacular, but most of all inspiring.

Steeped in history, aesthetically pleasing and criss-crossed by dozens of footpaths, the Pendle region is a well-trodden landscape with much to offer. We can learn and wonder about times gone by; how different its appearance would have been centuries ago when the majority of the views would have been obscured by dense woodland, which would in fact have made getting a good view a rare thing. The landscape lets us engage in a multitude of physical activities, whether hiking, birdwatching or something more extreme like climbing or paragliding, all are windows of opportunity to reconnect with nature – and in turn ourselves. The Pendle landscape allows us to experience the feeling of a much larger and more remote place than its location would suggest. Wild winds, exposure, and extensive views are aplenty while remaining in relative safety. Even on the remotest of moorland locations you're never too far from an open fire and a good pint.

PREVIOUS PAGE – Pendle emerges from the darkness as seen from Rylstone moor.
RIGHT – Snow-blasted and weather-ravaged hawthorn trees lead to one of Pendle Hill's most dramatic slopes: the north side as seen near Rimington, Ribble Valley.

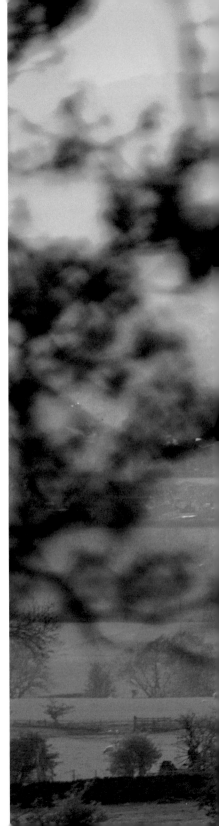

The unusual geography laid down by great rivers many millennia ago have resulted in a visual treat for the view-bagger and photographer alike. The multitude of smaller rolling hills offer a seemingly endless raft of vantage points from which to look for new horizons or to go on to explore the microvalleys and hedgerows so embedded in the landscape.

The area has a reputation for grey skies and rain. The saying goes 'if you can see Pendle Hill it's about to rain and if you can't see Pendle it is already raining'. This is absolute nonsense, no doubt conjured up by people who spend too long indoors and aren't actively engaging with the fresh air. England is part of an island which sticks its nose into one of the largest oceans on the planet. We therefore have a maritime climate, which means there is one thing you can be very certain of as far as the weather is concerned: change. Whatever it's doing, it won't last for long. This is a great opportunity for the hiker, nature enthusiast or landscape plodder; the conditions one can experience around Pendle are simply as good as anything you will see anywhere in the world.

Pendle has a well-publicised, rich and varied history which has much more breadth than just witches or the industrial revolution, both so fitting for the damp climate. It is a landscape that has inspired free thinkers in both politics and religion: from local suffragist Selena Cooper of Barnoldswick – one of four women selected to present the 'votes for women' campaign to the prime minister in 1910 – to well-known radical preachers like George Fox. Great writers, artists and athletes have also been inspired, such as Tolkien, who often visited Stonyhurst College which sits under Pendle's gaze. Modern paragliding athletes and a clutch of talented artists have all developed and bloomed in Pendle's shadow. Its location off the beaten track has always made for the perfect place where one can think outside the box and hone one's craft.

Right – Clitheroe Castle, built in the twelfth century and originally the property of the de Lacy family who first enclosed the region as a deer-hunting area.

Pendle's most famous claim to fame needs no introduction. Witch country dominates the themes of many things in the Pendle area, from beer to bus routes, pubs to paths and an array of local company logos. The generic visual of a bedraggled witch dressed in black flying on her broomstick is on the verge of being overused, although it has been noted that the X43 bus route 'the Witch Way' has a rather more *sassy* version these days, though bordering on objectification. You could certainly say that being the location for one of the most notorious witch trials in history has not been lost on the area! With the public celebration of the 400-year anniversary of the 1612 trials and a BBC documentary *The Pendle Witch Child*, the intrigue in our celebrated broomstick cruisers has ramped up considerably. The visual links between the landscape, the types of conditions it produces and all the clichés that come with witchcraft are easy to make. Images of wild old women with facial warts, ragged clothes and knotted hair flying around Pendle's summit on broomsticks is something that captures the collective imagination, fascinating people from far and wide. Perhaps this stereotype is born more from Hollywood than reality. It is great fun though, and the popularity of climbing Pendle around Halloween and the adjoining Blacko Tower – often mistaken for the infamous witches' meeting point, Malkin Tower – reached such levels of congestion that climbing the hill at Halloween was banned for a while in the 1990s and access to Blacko Tower has now been prohibited for many years.

The trial of twelve 'witches' saw the death of one in custody and the hanging of ten others. In 2012 a stunning installation piece by local artist Philippe Handford consisting of '1612' written on the side of the hill using special material was initially a hard sell, but proved to be a huge success giving the region coverage that a multimillion-pound marketing campaign could not compete with. Despite all this, there is little definitive information to be found about the witches.

LEFT – Pendle's aesthetics famously lend themselves to the theme of witchcraft. Hawthorn trees lead to Pendle Hill from Noggarth Top.

'It was an area fabled for theft, violence and sexual laxity, where the church was honoured without much understanding of its doctrines by the common people.'

– *The Pendle Witch-Trial 1612*, Rachel A.C. Hasted

The final line of this quote gives us perhaps the biggest clue as to what the real motives behind the witch trials were. Those of a country in uncertain times, aspiring lieutenants grasping their opportunity to progress up the ladder at the expense of some very unfortunate and mislabelled families that lived at the base of Pendle Hill. Not only was there the over-riding religious upheaval that was sweeping England at the time, but the general use of the word 'witch' to condemn any woman who transgressed the norms demonised and punished her to make others afraid to follow in an unruly woman's footsteps. You could argue that the roots of the term 'witch' and all the baggage that comes with it was simply ingrained social misogyny designed to repress the intellect of women and in turn, of course, keep the men in charge. Notice how a male sorcerer's title of 'wizard', 'alchemist' or 'warlock' carries no such stigma as the horrors we associate with the word 'witch'. Religion and misogyny would prove to be more powerful than any *actual* evidence in a court of law at that time.

One of the most shocking revelations of the trials was the conviction of Alice Nutter, a well-respected woman in the community from a relatively wealthy family who resided at Roughlee Hall. On Good Friday 1612 a great meeting was held at Malkin Tower of the friends and allies of the already-arrested Pendle witches being held at Lancaster Castle (not being in church on Good Friday was seen as an act of religious nonconformity). Once this meeting reached the ears of magistrate Roger Nowell, everyone suspected of involvement was rounded up – this included Alice Nutter. This was all based on the evidence of James Device who claimed to have been at the witches' meeting and named not only the motive of the meeting – to rescue the prisoners by blowing up the castle – but also

RIGHT – Ravens and crows are commonplace throughout the region, adding a sense of the sinister in the right light.

everyone therein. Alice Nutter was on the list. She made no statement at the trial other than 'Not guilty' and maintained her innocence until the end. Despite only very flaky evidence, Alice's fate was sealed on the gallows.

A Note from the Author – *Pendle is where I have lived all my life; playing in the fields, wastelands, mudpits and rivers around Brierfield as a child developed my adventurous spirit. Climbing the steep sides of the hill again and again in my twenties helped develop my fitness and endurance for wild conditions and much larger objectives I would go on to face. Photographing the hill and its surrounding satellites in my thirties developed my photography and taught me all the skills I required. Now in my forties, once again Pendle proves to be a source of inspiration re-igniting my passion and enthusiasm for photography as my creative career moves through its own highs and lows.*

Throughout this book I have had an intensive period chasing the light, looking for new angles and hoping for the morning mist, all in the name of the ultimate Pendle image, which of course doesn't exist. I have really tried to capture a more atmospheric mood that is true to the area and reflects many periods of Pendle's deep history – including the present.

When we think about Pendle we think about the area's most famous claim to fame – that of the witches. This is the overwhelming direction of the book: mist over the hills, babbling brooks, strange fungi growing in the damp, hidden valleys. It is easy to sense an air of mystery when observing Pendle and in the right conditions it's unequivocally a very spooky place to be.

I have sought out what few trees remain to try and conjure a feeling of its prior, more densely forested area, and chased the conditions to present Pendle at its most atmospheric. You could argue the most famous witch of all, Alice Nutter, just happened to be in the wrong place at the wrong time; perhaps to feel the true power of the witch country is simply a case of being in the right place at the right time.

Wonderfull
Discoveries

Four hundred years ago witchcraft was to some extent an accepted part of life, with rituals, healers and the prescription of potions and tinctures all part of the rural way. By contrast, the 'witch country' of today has little to no evidence of any actual witchcraft. Searching for any such activity could be viewed as futile in today's Pendle.

Occultism is the study of the occult or hidden wisdom. For the occultist, it is the 'truth' that must be sought, a deeper truth that exists beneath the surface. Perhaps this was the more benevolent motive behind the perceived witches' practices and intentions. The recent archaeological discovery of 'the witches' cottage' at the base of Pendle Hill in 2013 had a black cat within its walls, presumed to ward off evil spirits. Although you never know, perhaps the unfortunate feline just fell asleep at the wrong time in the wrong place. Any actual magic, astrology, spiritualism, extra-sensory perception is hard to identify in the Pendle region, at least at first glance … In this first chapter 'Wonderfull Discoveries' (incorrect spelling a reference to Thomas Potts's account of the 1612 trial) we can observe some of the atmospheric conditions that could be interpreted as more magical and astrological sights that may be interpreted as supernatural.

Witchcraft aside, what we will discover is that Pendle is so much more than just a hill surrounded by other nondescript smaller hills. Looking closely we will unearth a pantheon of detail not only in flora and fauna, but also fleeting moments – when the elements allow – of nature at its most spectacular. We can begin to understand why the area carried such a reputation of myth and legend and also why the fear of sorcery and magic was so rife.

Unlikely ice formations, rare lichens, forgotten streams, wild weather, weird fungi, fossilised sea life and misinterpreted towers, Pendle has it all …

PREVIOUS PAGES – The energy of Pendle Water was once harnessed to power the mills dotted across the area; the remaining waterfall is found parallel to the road in Roughlee village.
RIGHT – At first glance, there's nothing remarkable about this drystone wall, other than it is blocking the view towards Blacko Tower. Only after waiting here for a while for a shower to pass does a veritable Hanging Gardens of Babylon reveal itself in the form of some exotic, microcosmic and intricate lichen; some kind of *Cladonia* seen here doing its best impression of a Japanese bonsai tree.

'The wild and desolate parts of the parish of Whalley furnished a fitting scene for witch assemblies.'

– Lancashire Folk-Lore, John Harland and T.T. Wilkinson, 1867

Above – A bracket fungus thriving at the base of a mossy oak tree near Black Moss reservoirs. Even on the dullest of days, there's always something interesting to find and study. The layout is three different angles of the same subject.
Right – Searching high and low for points of interest. A water droplet is overcome by gravity from one of many icicles formed under the bridge of the road to Downham below Pendle's big end.

When the hard of winter comes we are treated to some intricate ice formations spotted here on a roadside hedge. Heavy rain caused the section of road to flood and the resulting spray and splash from the traffic coated the hedge with water. The plummeting temperatures did the rest. Aʙᴏᴠᴇ – Wild mushrooms grow on a tree stump in the plantation of fir trees at Ogden Clough.

Astrological sights around Pendle Hill; the Milky Way tries its best over the Pendle area on a clear night. No matter which side you choose the light pollution comes into shot, either from the urban corridor of Burnley and Pendle or that of the Ribble Valley. This would not have been the case a hundred years ago, and certainly towards the end of the sixteenth century a clear, moonless night over Pendle must have been a spectacular sight and one of great wonder to the locals of that time. Top Right – Villages and hamlets abound in the Ribble Valley. Bottom Right – The bright lights of Colne, Nelson and Brierfield.

'In every walk with nature one receives far more than he seeks.'

– John Muir

More bizarre fungi formations: *Polyporus squamosus*. Life never ceases to amaze as to where it can thrive. Fungus has many of the answers to the world's medical and environment problems. Perhaps one of its main advantages is its lack of need for any light; in fact the darker and danker, the better!

A spectacular sight that requires real intimacy with the subject found at Witches' Quarry, just north of Pendle Hill, Ribble Valley (*see also page 63*). These limestone rocks were formed in the Carboniferous period some 300 million years ago, when what was to become the Pendle area was located in the southern hemisphere in a more tropical climate. The warmer waters were rich with thousands of tiny molluscs and abundant marine life. Limestone is mainly composed of skeletal fragments of marine organisms such as coral, forams and molluscs. Normally the actual shapes of the fragments are no longer visible due to the pressure of the formation process. However at Witches' Quarry they have been fossilised in this extraordinary rock.

The area is exposed to some wild and spectacular weather which could easily be interpreted as a positive omen or equally an evil warning sign from higher beings or spiritual forces. When serendipity strikes and any given conditions just happen to follow a certain spell cast, we can start to understand how easy it is to believe in the power of witchcraft. Who knows what traditions or superstitious acts were regularly adhered to, then by chance a dark sky may form the following day. It doesn't take much to put two and two together and make five, interpreting cause and effect as that of your own doing. Just as Alison Device did, upon admitting she was a witch due to the poor fellow she attempted to cast a spell on by chance happening to have what was most likely a stroke at the same time.

Misconceptions and falsehoods can still be found today. It is still commonly thought that Blacko Tower or Stansfield Tower, built in 1890 by a local grocer 'to assist with the view', is in fact the famous meeting point of the witches: Malkin Tower. Unfortunately this is incorrect, which is a real shame as it fits the story so well!

Previous pages – Blacko Tower burning in the evening light. Opposite – Blacko Tower and the view to Pendle Hill experience four seasons in one day: a double rainbow, cloud bursts, hail, snow and sunshine. Conditions not uncommon – particularly in late winter or early spring.

Water is the substance that defines the area perhaps more than any other. The region's rise in elevation meets the full force of the warm yet moisture-laden gulf stream and prevailing westerlies of the Atlantic Ocean. ABOVE – Ominous rain clouds over Foulridge and Colne. RIGHT – Backlit cloudbursts from Witches' Quarry, near Downham.

Many assume the rise of Pendle Hill causes any rain clouds to unload their carriage over the landscape to the east. Resulting in a plentiful supply of water across the witch country. Its rivers and streams shape our landscape with many of the babbling brooks providing havens for the flora that thrive in a cold, dark and damp environment. The five reservoirs within the immediate proximity of the hill itself and another half dozen within close proximity add some tremendous beauty, inviting diverse wildlife to make it their habitats.

LEFT – Lower Foulridge Reservoir or Lake Burwain on a stormy morning, captured on a long exposure creating the motion-blurred effect of the current. ABOVE – Fallen branches wedged in the river feeding from Upper Black Moss Reservoir.

The multitude of major and minor watercourses make a massive contribution to the biological diversity found around Pendle. The oxygen-rich, pollution-free becks, brooks and larger watercourses support a thriving population of insect life and fauna as well as a variety of fish. TOP – Nature thriving in the dark, damp atmosphere – things growing on the things that grow. MIDDLE – The stream's flow polishes the rocks as the winter snows melt. BOTTOM – Interesting bark formations by Pendle Water. RIGHT – A microcosm of beauty found around this small stream, a tributary to Pendle Water, just to the east of Roughlee. The water level is nice and healthy as the winter snows melt, and as the dominance of the colour green would suggest the area sees little or no direct sunlight, making it the perfect habitat for mosses.

LEFT – Prolonged cold weather takes a grip on the Water Meetings in Blacko. The process of the surface freezing and then the water level dropping results in this spellbinding ice formation. OPPOSITE – Perhaps the area's most beautiful reservoir: Lake Burwain. A large body of water built in the eighteenth century as the main feed for the locks on the Leeds and Liverpool Canal as it reaches its highest point, and a great sanctuary for birdlife. Hundreds of seagulls sit on the water's surface amongst a symphony of chatter waiting for lift-off at first light (*see also page 117*).

Take to the Hills

In a world of processed food, processed social interactions and unprecedented levels of obesity there has never been a more important time to put your phone down, turn off the TV and get out into the hills. Even on the wildest of days you will never return with a sense of regret. In fact the opposite is true: you will always return from the hills recharged and invigorated, refreshed and reconnected – not just with nature – but with yourself.

Is it the fresh, unpolluted Lancashire air, the breathtaking views or the natural feel-good endorphins released into your system that give an overwhelming sense of wellbeing after any foray into the landscape? No doubt a combination of them all. It is not just your physical health that will benefit from getting out there, but your mental health too. Many recent studies have shown regular walks in the countryside to be more effective than antidepressants. Walking up and down Pendle will not resolve all the problems in your life or fix a broken heart, but it will help your mind find a state of serenity in which to resolve things in a more pragmatic way.

With the environment under increasing threat, looking after and respecting the land is also an important factor. It's hard to imagine a world without access to the outdoors and this right is taken as a common right – however only on the grounds that the basics are adhered to. You know what they are: pick litter up, keep dogs on leads, clean up after them, close gates, no fires etc. All very well-documented stuff. Try and imagine the landscape as an extension of your own property and you are responsible for its upkeep and will benefit from its preservation.

Let's celebrate and be inspired to get out there. Whether a toddler taking her first steps under her own steam, a fell runner testing endurance or just a Pendle summit addict who simply can't stay away. It doesn't matter how you get out there: you can fly, you can climb, you can do it on a bike or a horse. Whichever way you get outdoors, you're going to feel better, *without* recourse to witchcraft.

PREVIOUS PAGE – Rose Lee makes her way down Pendle Hill at three years of age. OPPOSITE – Local artist and mountain biking enthusiast Richard Davies takes to the hills with his eldest son Matt. Seen here enjoying one of the area's many bridleways, Gisburn Trail, which takes the high road over Weets Hill. FOLLOWING PAGE – Richard's youngest, Adam follows on at his own pace.

Doesn't matter how you do what you do in the hills. It's just that you do it. Sadly our connection with the landscape isn't what it would have been 400 years ago (relative to the population size), mainly due to the rapidly changing social and work environment. Isolation due to cars and computers, the breakdown of the traditional family unit and the all-powerful corporate media pumping our brains with endless ideals that can be achieved through buying stuff and eating junk. It would be helpful if they could get the message out to people that they should go for a walk in the green spaces every now and then; it's good for you and costs nothing. Until then, don't be thinking 'there's nothing to do outside'. On the contrary: everything you can do is outside.

Mountain-biking aficionado Richard Davies passes on his skills and passion for the outdoors to his sons Matt and Adam. An after-school ride on a summer's evening is all part of a rounded education. Gisburn Trail, Weets. OPPOSITE – Matt picks up some speed leaving Pendle in a blur.

'Small enough to still be considered a hill, but big enough to offer a mountain experience to the runner.'

– Mick Dobson, local fell runner

Pendle's rich variety of terrain makes it a favourite for fell runners. With hard climbs and long descents, everything is there for a challenging training session or a relaxed social run. Opposite – Fell runners Kerrie-Anne Bretherton, Meg and Mick Dobson making a rapid descent from the summit mists.

PREVIOUS PAGES – When the temperatures rise people flock to Pendle's trig point via all manner of means. Wonderful cotton grass can be found in large field-like patches on the summit plateau in the month of June. ABOVE – Simon Lee, a member of the Lancashire Youth Brass Band, plays 'The Last Post' on the hills above Nelson to coincide with the Pendle Hill *Poppies 1918* installation by Philippe Handford in conjunction with the 'Colne commemorates 1918' event (*see also page 142*). OPPOSITE – Start em young: Louis Lee makes an ascent of Pendle aged one and three quarters, spurred on by his mother and sister.

The Pendle Alps for a day. Not quite the deluxe powder conditions of Mount Fuji in Japan but a lifelong ambition achieved of some sort. The author shows his total lack of snowboarding ability on the big end. The snow was a little too hard and wind-sculpted, not to mention sparse. The blood pumped through the veins, sweat glands were in full action and adrenaline was released: mission accomplished. Very little snowboarding was completed and it really didn't matter. ABOVE FROM LEFT TO RIGHT – Wiping out, chilling out, checking the camera for the self-timer shots.

Witches' Quarry, a fabulous little climbing venue located in the Ribble Valley on Twiston Lane, east of Downham village. The unique and extraordinary rock gives superb short rock climbs that are at odds with the crag's loose and dirty appearance. Pendle lies on an interesting fault line geologically, with the hill itself being made of gritstone shale. Witches' Quarry just a mile or so to the north consists of much older hard limestone, formed millions of years ago by abundant marine life. First quarried for the limestone kilns to produce building materials and farming nutrients, now the remaining steep walls are used for challenge and recreation. Ever wonder what your bones might be doing in a few million years? Lancashire climbers Dave Sutcliffe and John Banny show us how it's done (see also page 33).

For some, a gentle stroll just won't cut it. World class paraglider and Lancastrian Jack Pimblett shows why he's currently ranked as the UK's number one acrobatic flyer. Jack has been taking tandem flights on Pendle with his father since the age of three and flying solo from fifteen. Seen here making the approach for a 'wingtip touching' trick on Mearley Moor, Pendle Hill. FOLLOWING PAGES LEFT – The 'wingtip touching' acrobatics in full execution. FOLLOWING PAGES RIGHT – Come fly with me: perfect conditions on a summer's evening on the Nick o' Pendle (*see also pages 136–137*).

Life in the clouds from Pendle Hill's summit plateau, the visionary vantage point more akin to views seen from high altitude mountain peaks. If there's thick fog in the valleys don't despair, as there's a good chance Pendle will be rising above it all. Strolling across the vast plateau of Pendle Hill is hard to beat.

Forest of Pendle

Much of the Pendle area – particularly to the east – was once a dark forest. Around the time of the witches in the late sixteenth century it would have been much more heavily vegetated than the landscape we experience now. The demise of the once forested lands is largely due to the demands of construction, fuel materials and farming. This means the foreboding forests of yesteryear have long since gone. However the trees and vegetation that have endured in the Pendle area still capture the spirit of the past. Many of these sparse trees have been left exposed and are shaped by the elements, preserving a certain charm unique to the area. While walking through the landscape it's easy to mistake twisted hawthorn trees for the bent, crooked posture of a witch, or the wild flowing branches of an ash tree for the bedraggled hair of an ancient sorcerer.

Left – Winter hits the edge of the post-war pine plantation above Newchurch in Pendle. Middle – A lonely tree stands exposed amongst the farmland above Jinny Lane en route to Newchurch. The dead wood: a final remnant of a once thriving hillside forest? Right – Sunburst through the misty upper canopy of an oak tree. Following page – A deciduous plot found just outside of the village of Fence. We can imagine that much more of the landscape would have taken this appearance centuries ago.

It would a take a time machine that could take us back around 5,000 years to find the existence of an actual Forest of Pendle. Much of the landscape would have been thickly wooded then, with only the most exposed summits an exception to this. These clearings would provide a welcome vantage point for ancient humans to survey the hunting ground. Taking in any type of vista 5,000 years ago must have been a pretty special experience. Shifting 2,000 years forward we would see the first real change upon the landscape as the climate became cooler and wetter; tree life could not flourish as it once did. Much of what could grow began to be removed by human intervention for grazing. This had a huge impact on the landscape and gave birth to the now familiar bare open moors, which in the grand scheme of time are relatively new. Moving forward another 2,000 years to around AD 1200 is when the name 'Forest of Pendle' first came into existence. The name emerges from the Norman conquerors, who set up areas known as forests to reduce habitation. The forests were areas of land set apart and 'subject to special conditions imposed by the royal will'. Exactly what that means – and more importantly what the true motivation behind this was – is unclear, however we can be sure it was not about naming a vast area of trees. Around this time pastoral development was also on the increase as well as the introduction of 'vaccaries', areas cleared of forestation to graze cows.

The well-known settlements of Newchurch in Pendle, Roughlee and Downham came into existence around 500 years ago. This would in turn have brought more human impact on the landscape – no doubt more clearing for fuel and construction materials. Which leads us to the seventeenth century and the Pendle witches. What exactly did the landscape look like 400 years ago? It's hard to be precise, somewhere between the very well manicured landscape we see today and that of the more barren lands of 3,000 years ago would be a good estimate. Obviously, the transport network would have been limited to cart tracks and secret paths or animal trails through the wooded areas. Boundaries of any type would have been less distinct than today and – importantly – one of the area's most distinctive features, the drystone wall, would not have existed at all. None of the pine forests which were all planted very recently (the 1920s), or the reservoirs, were in existence either.

What we can be sure of is that while there was no great forest, the pockets of woodland that did exist would have been much larger than those we see in today's Pendle landscape. This chapter is a collection of arborous snapshots in the hope of conveying a larger, somewhat enchanting wooded land.

'Pendle Forest swarms with witches. They burrow in the hill-side like rabbits in a warren.'

– The Lancashire Witches, William Harrison Ainsworth

ABOVE – Wild garlic abounds in the woodlands of Pendle. Sometimes referred to as ramsons it is proffered as
the cure for almost anything if you consult enough herbalists. No doubt a popular remedy of the Pendle witches.
PREVIOUS PAGE LEFT – Twisted and battered hawthorn trees cling to their existence amongst the predominately
pastoral lands, as seen just on from Noggarth Top.

ABOVE – A rare collection of trees in an exposed position on Downham Road looking totally bewitching. Winter mists blast the unprotected trees forming ice where leaves once hung. PREVIOUS PAGE RIGHT – The same group of exposed trees on a calmer winter morning, having been dusted by the snows through the night.

OPPOSITE – Witch country in all its glory. When the mist descends upon the forest you can almost see malevolent figures in the distance casting their spells. RIGHT – 'Crown shyness' on full display, a natural phenomenon where the trees respect each others' space. The changing hue in the sky is as the fog on one side of the forest clears revealing a bright blue sky.

Less than ten per cent of the Pendle landscape is now woodland with
sixty-five per cent being 'improved grasslands'. Most of the remaining
woodland today is found in the steep-sided cloughs or occasionally on
hillsides where the gradient is too severe for grazing. Two of the best
wooded areas are the south-east facing slope of the Roughlee valley
(*below*) where there is a reasonable gathering of tree life, a mixture of
broadleaf and firs, seen here in autumn. The other is found by Pendle
Water in Brierfield where amongst the new plantations glimpses of more
ancient scenes can be found. Here, an almost Tolkienesque tree,
unusually with no bark.

'At one point when I was on the trail and I'd been walking
for days on my own with my little dog, I did a double take
when I looked behind me because I thought there were
these women in black sat watching me among the trees.'

– Joe Hesketh, Pendle's residing witch and local artist

The above quote is from Pendle artist Joe Hesketh who walked the thirty-nine-mile 'Purgatory Trail'
that links the Forest of Pendle and Lancaster Castle as part of her research into the witch trials.
PREVIOUS PAGE LEFT – Spring mists enhance an ancient oak tree. PREVIOUS PAGE RIGHT – Hardy hawthorn
trees survive the prevailing winds below the Nick o' Pendle, Ribble Valley. OPPOSITE – Spooky spirits
emerge from a small woodland located at the top of Red Lane, Colne.

The Forest of Pendle plays the winter wonderland. The south-east facing slope of the Roughlee valley with its dense woodland in clear view. As seen from Blacko.

Forest of Pendle 89

A lone hawthorn tree dances over a spring lamb in the evening light below the Nick o' Pendle.

The early summer sun sets on a deforested land that became known as the Forest of Pendle.

Keepers of the Region

*'In some parts where I have travelled, where great and spacious wastes,
mountains, woods, forests and heaths are ...'*

– John Norden, a visitor to the north of England in 1602

Little had changed in the witch country for millennia, then over the past few centuries the forces of human impact sculpted the landscape into the forms, shapes and familiar sights of today. The advent of the population expansion and demand for the land's resources have stripped back much of the vegetation and hugely reduced the fauna that once roamed wild. The dominant force that shapes today's landscape is farming, followed by the water authorities with huge areas of pastoral and moorlands under their stewardship. A transformation from spacious wastes to well-kept cherished lands.

The area was first enclosed as a deer hunting area for the de Lacy family of Clitheroe, before development began for farming cattle in the thirteenth century, when the building of vaccary walls designated areas for grazing. Then at just about the time of the witch trials, the enclosures acts were brought in by parliament and over the next 300 years, what was once the common land was gradually divided up and legal property rights were created. Open fields were enclosed and the landscape changed into something much more familiar. The dominant feature for this partition of the land being drystone walls followed by laid hedges and some fencing.

Wildlife is still present – although not to the extent that it once would have been. Bears and wolves have long since been hunted out. The area is home to some prolific birdlife with Pendle Hill itself being a hotspot at certain times of year for keen ornithologists. Roe deer, foxes, and badgers can all be spotted if you are out early (or late) enough and are light enough underfoot so as not to scare them away. Rabbits, hares and grey squirrels are a much more common sight around the hills.

The local authorities help to promote tourism in the area as well as maintaining signposts, footpaths and access for an ever growing and enthusiastic community. The most recent development being the 'Lancashire Witches Walk'. Getting into our treasured little green lumps has never been so popular and is appreciated by the full diversity of the local population and increasingly from further afield.

There are artists inspired by the landscape expressing their passion in the form of writing, painting, photography and sculpture. 2012 saw the opening of Pendle's very first sculpture trail in Aitken Wood around a mile from the village of Barley.

This chapter celebrates not just the people behind maintaining the landscape and the aesthetics of well-cared-for lands, but also captures some fleeting moments from nature and acknowledges its crucial role in the ecosystem.

PREVIOUS PAGES – Domesticated and hungry, this particular breed of sheep, possibly a Blue Faced Leicester, is large and reasonably intimidating when in a large group, which they generally are. ABOVE – Philippe Handford, lead artist of the Pendle Sculpture Trail, makes regular visits to the trail to maintain the sculptures. FOLLOWING PAGES – Philippe Handford makes an inspection on his stunning piece *Reconnected 2* found on the Pendle Sculpture Trail in Aitken Wood.

ABOVE – *Reconnected 1* by local artist Philippe Handford found on the Pendle Sculpture Trail in Aitken Wood. OPPOSITE –
The best time to visit the wood is when the evening light floods through the trees. TOP LEFT – Tree bats, a curved wall titled
Gateway (Handford) and *Stone Pole* by Sarah McDade, just some of the many delights to be discovered on the trail.

Lesser seen contributors to the ecosystem; Left – Moorland heather provides an excellent sheltered habitat for our arachnid friends. An essential part of the ecosystem and the essence of the witch country in microcosmic form. Below – Hedgerows provide habitats for nearly eighty per cent of all woodland birdlife and around half of all mammals. This one is patched up with fencing and barbed wire. Previous pages left – Butterflies are becoming more scarce in the countryside; a rare sighting of the common copper. Previous pages right – Wasps. Despite their bad reputation we are better with them than without. Pollinating plants as they feed on the nectar, they are one of the many vital insects that keep nature ticking over.

The drystone wall, perhaps the most idiosyncratic feature of the northern English landscape, is in abundance throughout the Pendle area. This most identifiable artificial feature has gradually crept across the landscape over several stages of enclosure during the past few centuries. The majority of the well-divided landscape we see today is a result of the seventeenth-century enclosures act as much more of the land began to be used for farming.

Some say it was the French soldiers captured during the Napoleonic wars that built all the walls around Pendle, others say it was slaves, farmers, shepherds, farm labourers, soldiers or general labourers paid to do the work. Whoever it was, what we can be sure of is the monumental amount of effort it took to construct the miles and miles of walls we see today; it was truly a phenomenal feat.

Depending on the height and width of the wall it takes around one tonne of stone for every metre of wall. Naturally all that stone didn't just happen to be laying in neat rows, the transport of materials to often unforgiving territory is something in itself. Then there's the beauty, improvisation and fantastic simplicity of building a structure made from locally available stone (and nothing else other than sweat, graft and bruised fingertips). The stones are arranged in a particular pattern so that they lock themselves together to create a solid structure that can last for hundreds of years.

Nowadays maintaining the walls is an expensive process as cheap labour is a thing of the past as the skills required gradually wash away with the next generation. It can cost up to £100 per metre to build, and a good waller can construct between two to four metres in a day, depending on the size of wall and proximity of the stone.

There's something incredibly organic about these so obviously man-made features. It's not just how naturally they blend with the landscape, but also they provide a habitat for a great variety of animals. Shrews, field mice, voles, stoats, hedgehogs, bats, toads and slow-worms all make their homes among the wall, and hares will scrape a hollow at the base of a wall where it will remain sheltered from the worst of the elements. Many birds too, such as the robin, wheatear, redstart and the occasional small owl, have been known to occupy larger gaps, with mosses, lichens and ferns favouring the outside of the walls. Truly a natural fit.

Left – Retired local baker and serial collector of walling and hedgelaying trophies, seventy-four and still going strong: Ralph Lee. Above – The drystone wall, rather than one single row of stones is in fact two rows, with the middle filled in. Following pages – The view from Weets Hill towards Pendle. Even in demise, the drystone wall maintains its aesthetics if not its function.

Above – The much larger fields of the Ribble Valley are generally divided by hedgerows and fencing. Opposite – The majority of the farmland is used to cultivate grass; Pendle walls in disrepair; spring lambs; cattle feeding station at sunset.

Pendle Hill is a migratory passage site for some very interesting species of bird. Its large summit grass meadows and clear elevation make it an obvious pitstop for winter dwelling from an aerial perspective. Opposite we see the much-pursued snow bunting; an annual winter visitor and double-passage migrant. These are either females or juveniles judging by the plumage and, as ever, travelling at some speed.

The snow bunting is without doubt the toughest small bird on our planet. It is one of only three birds to be sighted at the North Pole. The others being seabirds – kittiwake and fulmar. Basically it's as tough as old boots, but do remember to keep your distance – especially when they're spotted in a large intimidating flock. Please never harass or disturb the birds.

They breed in the Arctic in summer but migrate south for winter to circumnavigate the northern temperate zone including Canada, northern USA, northern Asia, northern Europe, and Pendle where the birds feed on the Molinia grass found on the summit plateau.

This shot (opposite) was captured around the end of November amongst a flock of about a dozen, seen diving down the eastern slopes around the main path.

ABOVE – A pied wagtail feeds on the moss and lichen growing on a drystone wall. A meadow pipit on the summer ferns of Pendle Hill. RIGHT – Not all the prolific bird life in the area is as well travelled as the snow bunting; here we see a flock of seagulls travelling inland where the farmland provides rich feeding grounds. FOLLOWING PAGE – A wingbeat symphony of starlings gives a magnificent display in front of Pendle Hill. As seen walking from Newchurch in Pendle to Upper Ogden Clough.

ABOVE – A kestrel dive-bombs a much larger bird of prey, possibly a buzzard. The area is the habitat for many birds of prey, however spotting them is not so easy. OPPOSITE – Bird activity is at its highest around dawn; the hundreds of seagulls captured here are taking off from one of the area's most popular breeding grounds, Foulridge Reservoir (*see also page 40*).

ABOVE TOP – Long grasses in the marshlands of Pendle. BOTTOM LEFT – Over time the land sculpts the once-straight wall into something more artistic. BOTTOM RIGHT – Curlews in the fog. OPPOSITE – Mallards take flight from the wetlands where they come to mate. FOLLOWING PAGES – VR panoramic image displaying the densely populated 'urban corridor'; approximately 140,000 people reside between Burnley to Colne to the south of Pendle Hill.

Pendle Hill

'A deep purple crept out of the gullies …
It crept up to meet the sky. It crept down to
engulf the trees. It spread, and it deepened, till
all the hill was one vast brooding thing.'

– *Mist Over Pendle*, Robert Neill

Pendle Hill, unique amongst all of England's hills, a beacon on the Lancashire skyline drawing all that live around her to experience the joys and delights the great hill can offer. Hiking to the summit to revel in the expansive views on all sides of the hill is at an all-time level of popularity. The relative prominence of its eastern and northern slopes amounts to something well beyond what its humble height would suggest. One may take in the Yorkshire Dales and Lake District to the north, and Blackpool Tower and the Irish Sea to the west. To the east the next highest point lies among the Ural Mountains or Russian steppes some 3,000 miles away. On any given weekend an encouragingly diverse mix of ethnicities and people of all shapes, sizes and ages can be seen bounding from the lay-by at its base or from a thronging car park at Barley where droves of enthusiastic walkers head for the hill, eager to feed from its energy. Often grey and underwhelming in appearance, the modest 557 metres of Pendle Hill's highest point can sometimes sink into obscurity. However when the morning light shines and the mists clear Pendle shows why it is the jewel in the county's crown with natural wonders and scenes of a truly spectacular nature. The seductive siren in its magical mists and strange cloud cover makes the perfect backdrop for the area's famous history, only enhancing the weird and wonderful tales, myth, legend and folklore of the witch country.

OPPOSITE – First light strikes the hill through the morning spring mist as the author casts a shadow from Mountain Top. A partial fogbow and a Brocken spectre add to the magic of this image.
PREVIOUS PAGES – Pendle Hill in a purple haze of winter, 'one vast brooding thing'. The Lancashire landmark that has inspired so much more than tales of witchcraft over the centuries.

After hundreds of ascents of the hill, its lure only grows stronger as new light and conditions shape an eternal range of breathtaking guises. If you are under any doubt as to why Pendle is the world's greatest hill, simply look at the meaning behind its name. 'Pen' being the Celtic word for hill, 'dun' or 'dhul' from Saxon times means 'hill', and then our more recognisable modern term … 'hill', all adds up to 'hill, hill, hill'! Which says a lot about just what a magnificent hill it is.

Immovable and ever present to the people that have lived around the hill for centuries, it dominates the landscape, and can be seen from miles around on all sides with its familiar and unmistakeable profile and shape. Its classic curve with the slight humpback easily makes it Lancashire's most recognisable sight. As you move round to the northern sides it takes on a slightly more uniform shape, almost Ayre's Rock-like in profile. From the north and west it's almost an exact mirror image of how it appears from the eastern side without the humpback – the wrong way around, depending on which side you are most familiar with. Its profile makes it hard to grasp exactly what kind of shape Pendle is, as it appears to have a very similar slope from many angles. This is because the hill is in fact more like a horseshoe in shape when viewed from the air.

Whichever side you see Pendle from history has shown it has an ever-present power to draw people to it, famous not just for witches but a source of such inspiration. Having ascended the hill in 1652 George Fox had a vision which prompted him to found the Quaker movement. Having seen the great hill George notes in his autobiography: 'I was moved of the Lord to go up to the top of it.' Just ten years later well-known local mathematician Richard Towneley conducted some early barometric experiments at Pendle, making good use of its vertical scale.

The Victorian era heralded the first real age of tourism, resulting in a trainline up the east slope very close to where the main path lies today. The earliest evidence of human interaction with the hill is that of Bronze Age burial sites near the summit. In the current age, the relatively huge numbers of people that live around the hill result in more pairs of feet on the paths than ever before, with estimates of around 300,000 people climbing the hill every year.

OPPOSITE – The brooding mass of Pendle's big end comes into view like the prow of an enormous ship gliding into a dock.

On the face of it, Pendle Hill is nothing but a mass of shale laid down by great rivers which carried the eroded deposits of mountains many millennia ago. The course of time and a rich history has left us with something much more intangible, a spiritual home, a place of freedom.

This final chapter is a pictorial ode to the hill's multitude of forms and moods throughout the year, and testament to how our lives can be enriched by nature's subtleties. Being away from the mainstream and a little off the map is something that has always been in Pendle's favour – and is reflected in the people drawn to it.

'There is no hill in England like Pendle Hill.'

– *The Lancashire Witches*, William Harrison Ainsworth

Above – The village of Barley situated in the heart of the witch country, nestled in the rolling landscape around Pendle Hill.
Following pages – The immovable mass that is Pendle Hill – she has seen it all. This image is a merge of two photographs of the same view: a sunny autumn morning and a moody winter's morning as the bad weather approaches.

Above – The verdant pastures of the nutrient-rich limestone of the Ribble Valley in scorching summer.
Opposite – Contrasting with the gritstone wetlands to the east. As the summer approaches, the evening light begins to creep across the hill's northern slopes.

Above – A common sight on Pendle Hill: the skylark, seen here doing its renowned song-flight during which the bird rises almost vertically with rapid wingbeats before parachuting down. This is done to advertise its territories. The nests are hollows found amongst short vegetation in the ground. Left – Taking flight from Mearley Moor on the west side of Pendle Hill, a popular paragliding site when the north-west wind blows (*see also pages 64–67*).

ABOVE – Superb winter views from Pendle's eastern slopes looking directly east; the next highest point lies among the Ural Mountains in Russia some 3,000 miles away. OPPOSITE – Pendle Hill's 'big end' as seen from Twiston Moor, one of the most spectacular points from which to view the hill. At a mere 557 metres above sea level Pendle is nothing special in terms of actual height however its vertical scale of nearly 400 metres from the surrounding land is what makes it so impressive. FOLLOWING PAGES – One of the most commanding views of Pendle Hill is from its northern side, viewed here just north of Rimington in the Ribble Valley on a winter's evening.

Above – Pendle Hill *Poppies 1918* installation by Philippe Handford in conjunction with 'Colne commemorates 1918', taken during a heatwave on the summer solstice.
Just the poppy heads remain after a few days of strong winds on the hill removed part of the original installation (*see also page 58*). Right – From a certain angle,
Pendle has almost perfect symmetry, as seen here from the road to Downham, sporting a peaked cap of winter cloud.

ABOVE – The almost lime green of May at Pendle's base. Even the wetland grasses can't help but be inspired by Pendle's distinctive shape. The waters flow from Pendle Hill. OPPOSITE – The verdant Ribble Valley in late spring contrasts sharply with the rugged moorland grasses of the hill. Limestone soils against gritstone shale. Pendle's soft sedimentary rock makes it like a huge sponge, absorbing rainfall and holding the water within its mass. The occasional landslip can occur when the levee breaks, with the largest evidence of this type of erosion being on the big end where a huge indent on the hill's side can be seen. Natural springs also occur at several points around the hill.

'The dearest and grandest little old hill in the world.'

– Daniel Scanlin, local photographer

R<small>IGHT</small> – One of nature's greatest illusions, the fogbow – also known as a white rainbow. How can a perfect arch of fog be formed in the air? It can't. Similar to a rainbow, the arch only appears relative to where you are stood, the Brocken spectre of light in accordance to the angle you are looking from gives the appearance of the perfect arch. There is, in fact, the same amount of moisture (fog) across the whole scene. Sights like this could only confirm that witchcraft is at work in the area! The image on the following pages was captured thirty minutes later.

A rare cloud inversion closes in around Pendle Hill.
Spring is the most likely time to see this phenomenon,
caused by the difference in day and night temperatures combined with low winds and plenty of rainfall
prior to the event. ABOVE – Snow buntings and walkers
alike revel in the conditions.

Cotton grass flourishes in the summertime on Pendle Hill's summit plateau.

Walkers dwarfed by Pendle's immovable mass.

154

PREVIOUS PAGES – The classic view of Pendle Hill as you emerge from the steep road from Newchurch in Pendle before dropping down to Barley, captured here on a winter's morning during a brief clearing from a snowstorm. OPPOSITE – Winter sunset behind the hill's sleeping silhouette. LEFT – Lapwings in mating season around the base of Pendle's big end on a misty morning in early spring, captured during some spectacular flying.

… and in those fleeting moments when the weather clears, a window into another world appears. Not just one of clearer skies and glimpses of views that seem magnified, but one that creates an atmosphere more akin to an aerial flight, a world in the clouds. The hill's position on the map makes it the site of first impact for the prevailing weathers from the west. Scenes here are from a bracing winter's morning that soon had hands numb and face aching in the freezing winds – but what spectacular sights. At first light, an iridescence plays around Pendle's eastern slope before the view is lost completely and the landscape is engulfed by the inevitable downpour. ABOVE – The views to the north are sublime, a snow-capped Ingleborough is lit by first light. FOLLOWING PAGES – Pendle's unique character remains a refuge from the world and is regarded by many as their spiritual home, no longer viewed as a wild and lawless region – at least not officially. Was that a surveillance helicopter flying past during the capture of that image … (look closely into the sky to the right).

Acknowledgements

A special thanks to my family, friends and colleagues who have been so supportive, inspirational and encouraging. Without them this book may just be another potential idea in a notebook. From editors to spell checking, helping with photoshoots or just being there to tell me to keep going, I send much love and gratitude to you all. In no particular order – Mum and Dad, Elyse Baril-Guérard, Philippe Handford, Aaron Mooar, Joe Hesketh, Moorhouses Brewery, Helen Hartley, Mark Sutcliffe, Richard, Matt and Adam Davies, Kerrie-Anne Bretherton, Mick Dobson, Simon, Rose and Louis Lee, Jack Pimblett, John Banny, David Sutcliffe, Max Bretherton, James Stirzaker, Simon Lees, Dave Mycroft, and Jon Barton and all at Vertebrate Publishing.

A huge thank you to everybody that pledged any amount to the Kickstarter campaign. The support was fantastic and reassuring that my passion for Pendle is shared with so many – Mark Lee, Freddie Lee, Sam Lee, Mark Sutcliffe, Chrissy Brown, Lesley Dearden, Rebecca Mitchard, Paul Wheeler, Michael Ryan, Mick Dobson, Gail and Steve, Jonathan Sutterby, Robert Lovell, Steve Monks, Dave Ehlen, John Osborn, Andrea Wilkinson, Nicholas Oliver Livsey, Rob Browne, John Richmond, Mick Warn, Dominic Makin, Alex Nail, Alun Davies, Luke Gaskill, Roi Croasdale, Fiona Ritchie, Guy Richardson, Jo Kaye, Libby Holden, Ben Osborn, Alex Ekins, Sheard Sumner, Peter and Wendy Stobbs, Rachel Fryers, Matt Stoddon, James Davies, Ed Bailey, Dave Rowell, Rowena Kirk, Michelle Harland, Derrick Wroe, Marton Sasvari, Magda and Edith Wilkinson, Cheryl Davies, Matt Wilcock, Claire and Rob, Kev, Janice Weatherill Timmins, Matthew Troilett, Nicola McCoy, Jon Barton, David Toon, Malcolm, Graham Hill, Lisa Grant, Alan Birtwell, Scott Ribble, Darren, Matt, Eric and Margaret Bushby, Hannah Collingridge, Simon Lees, John Altringham, Paul Flynn, Tracy Cokill, Chamu Narayana, Mark Naughton, Steve Laycock, Alice Hydes, Mark Tait, Lindsey Houlding, Yadin Flammer, Simon Garvey, Broseph, Steve Bull, Sharon Christodoulou, Brian Sainter, Lyne Guérard, Fiona Lewis, Elizabeth Murphy, Hilthart Pedersen, Jonathan Andrew Nixon, Captain David R.J. McKinlay, Stephen Johnson, Dave and Heather Shaw, Jessica, Chris Bryan, Tim Garland, Sir Twonkalot, Konstantinos Marinopoulos, David A. James, Wendy Millar, Chris Reid, Stephen Hampshire, David Redpath, Lorraine Clarke, John and Maggie Wright, Bradley Jackson, Nicola and Mark Nuttall, Kerrie Bretherton, Alan Scowcroft, Chas and Kelly, Susan Brown, Jean Baril, Lee Metcalfe, Nick Wharton, Mark Sutcliffe, Sally and Miles, David Reeves, Ian Miller, Andrea Moustacas, Geneviève Baril-Guérard, Andréane Richard-Denis, Rob Johnson, Nicky Rourke, Tommy Brindle, Ant Carysforth, Kelvin Wilkinson, Joel Freeman, Janet Wilkinson, and Nick and Janine Herd.